Best wishes

Ey- ♥

Taos - summer
1983

Dora-Kaminsky Crespaul - Fenn Gallery
St Johns College

FECHIN: THE BUILDER

BY EYA FECHIN
IN COOPERATION WITH MOSES PORTER

LIMITED FIRST EDITION OF 3,000 COPIES

FECHIN: THE BUILDER — LIMITED FIRST EDITION OF 3,000

PUBLISHED IN 1982 BY EYA FECHIN
P.O. BOX 20, SAN CRISTOBAL, NEW MEXICO 87564

THIS BOOK WAS PRODUCED ENTIRELY WITHIN NORTHERN NEW MEXICO.

DESIGN AND PRODUCTION
MOSES PORTER/GREEN CHILI DESIGNWORKS — SANTA FE, NEW MEXICO

PHOTOGRAPHY
ROBERT NUGENT — SANTA FE, NEW MEXICO

TYPOGRAPHY, PRINTING, AND BINDING
BLUE FEATHER PRESS — SANTA FE, NEW MEXICO

An acknowledgement of gratitude and appreciation is due the Fechin Institute for their cooperation in contributing to the successful completion of this book.

The Fechin Institute is a cultural-educational, non-profit foundation (approved by the IRS March 30, 1981), striving to present and develop Fechin's unique approach to learning, teaching, and creating.

The Institute has leased the Fechin house and studio in Taos, New Mexico as a center for activities. The property is now a registered cultural site of New Mexico and is listed on the National Register of Historic Places (1979). There is a library and archives on the premises accessible for research purposes. The Institute is available to collectors, students, and dealers regarding accurate information on the life and work of Nicolai Fechin; authentification of his works; consultation on restoration and conservation of his drawings, paintings and sculpture. A permanent file of Fechin's work as well as a file on copies and forgeries is being added to continually.

Presently, the Institute is planning exhibitions, lectures and international exchange programs and is also cooperating with individuals and publishers of new books on Nicolai Fechin.

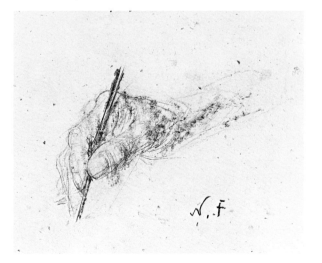

Nicolai Fechin – Chronology

1881	Born in Kazan, Russia, December 9th. (Old Julian calendar, November 26th).
1895	Enters newly opened Kazan Art School.
1900	Graduates from Kazan Art School, is accepted into the Art Academy in Petrograd (Leningrad).
1903	Goes on two summer trips along the South Enisei River in Siberia with an engineer-geologist.
1908	Becomes instructor at the Kazan Art School. Graduates from Art Academy with top honors and travels through Europe. Is invited to enter international exhibits.
1910	Participates in first American exhibit, Carnegie Institute in Pittsburgh, Pennsylvania.
1913	Marries Alexandra Belkovitch.
1914	Birth of only child, daughter Eya.
1923	August 1st, arrives in New York, USA, and lives there 4 years.
1926	Summer visit to Taos, New Mexico.
1927	Moves to Taos.
1931	Obtains U.S. citizenship.
1933	Divorced by Alexandra. Goes to New York for winter and then moves to Southern California.
1936	Travels in Mexico.
1938	Travels with friend Milan Rupert to Japan, Java, Bali.
1948	Buys the studio in Santa Monica, California.
1955	Special collectors' exhibit simultaneously in La Jolla Art Center and San Diego Art Museum.
	October 5, dies quietly in his sleep in his Santa Monica studio.
	December 20, only grandchild, daughter, Nicaela born.
1961	1st book on Fechin, Hammer Galleries in New York, text by Harold McCracken, (out of print).
1975	Summer, book on Fechin by G. Mogilnekova, published in Leningrad, USSR, (out of print).
	Winter, book on Fechin by M. Balcomb, E. Fechin, Northland Press, Flagstaff, AZ, (out of print).
1976	Exchange exhibits with USSR.
	Fechin ashes returned to Kazan by daughter and grand-daughter.
1979	Fechin house becomes State Historical Site, listed in the National Register of Historic Places.
1981	The Fechin Institute is organized and approved, and begins to use the Fechin house for educational-cultural activities.
	June-August, Centennial Exhibition, Montana Historical Society, Helena, Montana.
	September, Centennial Exhibition in Fechin House, Taos, New Mexico.
	October, American Indian Scholarship Fund, Inc. benefit in Fechin house-studio.
	December 9, Centennial show and conference in the Fine Arts Museum, Kazan, USSR.
1982	August, Bennett Wade, sculpture exhibition, Fechin studio.
	September 25, Fechin exhibition in the house. Printing of book "Fechin: The Builder".
	October, American Indian Scholarship Fund, Inc. benefit.

Awards and exhibits are too numerous to list here.

STEPPING INTO THE FECHIN HOUSE IS AN
EXTRAORDINARY EXPERIENCE. EVERYWHERE
ONE LOOKS, CARVED UNDULATING FORMS
ALMOST CRY OUT TO BE TOUCHED SO THAT
THEIR BEING MIGHT BE FULLY KNOWN.
THE HARMONY AND BALANCE ARE FELT AS
WELL AS SEEN — THE HOUSE "SINGS" FOR
YOU. A RUSSIAN HOUSE EVOLVED OUT OF
NEW MEXICO MUD. A BLACKSMITH, A
CARPENTER...INDIANS, SPANISH, ANGLOS,
WORKED HARD AND HAPPILY ALONGSIDE
THE MASTER ARTIST...NICOLAI FECHIN.

FECHIN: THE BUILDER

THE MASTER BUILDER STOOD BACK AND SURVEYED HIS WORK AND IT WAS GOOD! HE RAISED HIS AXE IN TRIUMPH AND FLUNG IT INTO THE QUIET WATERS OF LAKE ONEGA SHOUTING "THERE HAS NEVER BEEN, IS NOT, AND NEVER WILL BE SUCH ANOTHER!"

THERE ROSE BEFORE THE BUILDERS, SILHOUETTED AGAINST THE NORTHERN SKY OF KIZHI ISLAND, OUT OF THE DARK EARTH, THE CHURCH OF TRANSFIGURATION. LIKE A GIANT FIR TREE IT STOOD, MASSIVE WITH ITS 22 SUPERIMPOSED ONION-SHAPED DOMES ON A PYRAMIDAL ROOF, RESOUNDING IN ITS GLORY OF WOOD. THE YEAR WAS 1714 AND IN KEEPING WITH ANCIENT RUSSIAN TRADITION THE PRINCIPAL TOOL WAS THE AXE. THE INTRICACIES OF WOOD BUILDING WERE DONE WITHOUT THE USE OF NAILS OR EVEN THE AID OF A SAW. THE INTERIOR IS A MARVEL OF CARVING AND GILDING, THE ICONOSTASIS A JOYOUS FRAMEWORK FOR THE ICONS.

ACCORDING TO CONTEMPORARY ACCOUNTS, ANOTHER MARVEL OF WOOD, THE CARVED ORNAMENT OF THE OLD TIMBER PALACE (17TH CENTURY) IN THE VILLAGE OF KOLOMENSKOE WAS OF SUCH OUTSTANDING SPLENDOUR THAT IT WAS KNOWN AS THE "EIGHTH WONDER OF THE WORLD."

BUILDERS IN OLDEN TIMES WERE MOSTLY ANONYMOUS. THE ARCHITECTURAL WONDERS WERE A GROUP EFFORT, EVERY STROKE OF THE AXE CONTRIBUTING ESSENTIAL DETAILS TO THE WHOLE. THE ARCHITECTS, THE CARPENTERS, THE CARVERS, THE TREE CUTTERS, THE ARTISTS, THE LEAST OF THE LABORERS, WERE ALL "BUILDERS."

THE BUILDERS UNDERSTOOD THE "SOUL" OF THE WOOD, THE BEAUTY AND VARIETY OF ITS STRUCTURE, THE COLORING AND CHARACTER OF DIFFERENT TIMBERS. THE THIRST FOR THE

BEAUTIFUL WAS UPON THEM AND THE LONGING TO UNIFY WITH THE EARTH AND ALL ITS CREATURES. AND THE WOODED LAND, THE PRIMEVAL FOREST, BECAME THE NURSERY OF RUSSIAN CULTURE. THE RIVERS WERE THE HIGHWAYS FOR TRADE AND FOR COMMUNICATION WITH THE WORLD.

THE MATERIAL STRUGGLE AND FASCINATION WITH A HARSH ENVIRONMENT — THE EXTREMES OF WEATHER, BEARS, INSECTS, FEARS OF FIRES — CONTRIBUTED TO THE AROUSAL OF IMAGINATION, PASSION FOR BEAUTY AND DESIRE TO FIND A DESTINY. AS THE BEAUTY OF THE CHURCHES EMPHASIZED THE HUMAN SPIRIT, SO ALSO GREW THE NEED TO MAKE THE SMALL ARTICLES OF LIVING CARVED, PAINTED, SHAPED IN BRIGHTNESS — CHAIRS, TABLES, CUPBOARDS, DISHES, THE DOORS AND WINDOWS OF THE HUTS, GATES AND BARNS — ALL FELT THE TOUCH OF THE BUILDER'S HANDS. IT WAS MUCH LATER THAT LEO TOLSTOY SAID: "A RUSSIAN WITH NOTHING BUT AN AXE COULD BUILD A HOUSE OR SHAPE A SPOON."

GREAT WAS THE LOVE FOR WOOD. IT WAS ABUNDANT, FAMILIAR THROUGH MANY CENTURIES OF USE. THE AXE SYMBOLIZED THE MATERIAL STRUGGLE — THE ICON, THE SPIRITUAL EXULTATION. THE AXE COULD FASHION AN ICON AND PROTECT ONE FROM THE ENEMY. IN THE WILD FORESTS AND IN THE FIELDS, WHEREVER THE AXE WENT, THE SCYTHE AND THE PLOW AND THE BEE-KEEPER FOLLOWED...AND THE WILDERNESS WAS SETTLED BY HUMANS.

THE MOVEMENT NORTH HAPPENED DURING 1157-74 AND SAW THE RISE TO DOMINANCE OF THE "FOREST LAND," THE VOLGA-OKA RIVERS HEARTLAND. BEFORE THAT, THE "MOTHER OF RUSSIAN CITIES" WAS KIEV, FROM PRINCE VLADIMIR IN 988 TO THE MONGOL INVASION IN 1240. HERE OCCURRED THE ADOPTION BY THE RUSSIANS OF THE BYZANTINE (CONSTANTINOPLE) ARTISTIC FORMS AND A SENSE OF DESTINY OF THE BYZANTINE "SECOND GOLDEN AGE." WITHIN THE ORNATE AND STYLIZED BYZANTINE HERITAGE, KIEVAN RUSSIA DEVELOPED TWO DISTINCTIVE ATTITUDES WHICH GAVE THE INITIAL DIRECTION TO RUSSIAN CULTURE — DIRECT SENSE OF BEAUTY AND A PASSION

FOR SEEING SPIRITUAL TRUTH IN CONCRETE FORMS. THERE WAS A PROFOUND SENSE OF HISTORY, THE DESIRE FOR ROOTS, THE COMPELLING URGE OF DESTINY.

AN IMPORTANT OUTCOME FOR RUSSIA OF THE MONGOL INVASION ACROSS THE EURASIAN STEPPE IN THE 13TH CENTURY WAS THAT THE ONCE DISTANT FOREST REGIONS OF THE NORTH BECAME THE MAIN CENTER OF AN INDEPENDENT ORTHODOX CULTURE. THE GEOGRAPHICAL FOCUS CHANGED FROM THE DNIEPER RIVER TO THE UPPER VOLGA. THE CHARACTERS, EVENTS AND ARTISTIC FORMS OF KIEVEN TIMES DOMINATED THE CHRONICLES AND EPICS WHICH ASSUMED THEIR FINAL SHAPE IN THE CREATIVE MEMORY OF THE NORTH. CULTURE BECAME, ONE OF CONCRETE SIGHT AND SOUND, RATHER THAN ABSTRACT WORDS AND IDEAS. NOT ONLY WERE SAINTS SAID TO BE VERY LIKE THE HOLY FORMS ON THE ICONS, BUT THE WORD FOR EDUCATION — OBRAZOVANIYE — SUGGESTS "BECOMING LIKE THE FORMS."

THE ICONS BEGAN TO HUMANIZE DIVINE AUTHORITY, ESPECIALLY THE IMAGES OF THE VIRGIN. SHE BECAME THE QUEEN OF HEAVEN, DIVESTING HERSELF OF HER REGAL ROBES AND COMING FORTH FROM HER CHURCH TO PREACH CHRISTIANITY IN THE STREETS. SHE WAS SEEN AS NOT ONLY A CELESTIAL IMAGE, BUT FERTILE AS THE EARTH, THE RUSSIAN ETERNAL WOMANHOOD, MOTHER OF GOD, AND THE MOTHER FIGURE OF GREAT RUSSIA. RUBLEV (1370-1430) WAS CONSIDERED THE SUPREME ARTIST, THE PAINTER OF MAGIC ICONS.

THE ICONOSTASIS IS THE FRAMEWORK IN THE INTERIOR OF ORTHODOX CHURCHES WHICH HOLDS THE ICONS. IT FORMS A "SCREEN OF ICONS" SEPARATING THE PRIEST'S SANCTUARY FROM THE PEOPLE. AND THE GATES (OR DOORS) THROUGH WHICH THE PRIEST COMES FORTH TO BLESS AND "FEED" THE MULTITUDES IS PART OF THE CARVED ICONOSTASIS. PEOPLE LEARNED TO LOOK NOT FOR REALITY, BUT FOR "SPIRITUAL HARMONY IN ART." EVEN IN THE SMALLEST COUNTRY CHURCHES, THE ICONOSTASIS ARE WORKS OF ART. FROM CITY MANSIONS TO PEASANT HUTS, WOOD WAS USED WITH GREAT IMAGINATION. DURING THE 17TH

CENTURY DISTINCTIVE FEATURES OF ARCHITECTURE AND ART BEGAN TO MOVE TOWARD ASSYMETRY. AN ASTONISHING AMOUNT OF DIVERSE FORMS, COLORS, SHAPES WERE MAGICALLY BLENDED INTO HARMONY. ASSYMETRY GAVE FASCINATING LIFE, INTIMACY, AND ORGANIC ROOTS FOR A FREE FLOW OF IMAGINATION.

THIS BRIEF PRELUDE ABOUT RUSSIAN ARTS, AND ESPECIALLY THE PROFOUND INVOLVEMENT WITH WOOD, IS MEANT TO HELP UNDERSTAND FECHIN'S HERITAGE AND HIS NEED TO BUILD SUCH A HOUSE AS HE DID IN TAOS. THE ARCHITECTURAL ASSYMETRY IS THERE. EVERY DOOR AND WINDOW IS DIFFERENT, YET ALL ARE IN SUBTLE HARMONY WITH THE WHOLE. THE MARK, NOT OF THE SIMPLE AXE, BUT OF THE ADZE IS THERE ON EVERY BOARD AND BEAM, BECAUSE FECHIN LOVED THE TEXTURE IT PROVIDED. THE ADZE, A VERY SHARP INVERTED AXE, WAS USED TO FINISH BOARDS BEFORE THE METAL PLANE WAS INVENTED AND TAKES CONSIDERABLE SKILL (AND EVEN COURAGE!) TO PROPERLY SWING THE TOOL AND OBTAIN A SMOOTH, EVEN SURFACE AS YOU STRADDLE THE BOARD. THE UNDERSTANDING OF THE "SOUL" OF THE WOOD IS THERE.

THIS IS "FOLK ART," THE PEASANT'S DESIRE FOR BEAUTY AND SPIRITUAL FULFILLMENT. IT DIFFERS GREATLY FROM THE ELEGANTLY FINISHED CABINET WORK OF EUROPE AND OTHER COUNTRIES WHERE THE WOOD IS SUPERBLY USED WITH COMPLETE CONTROL OF THE MATERIAL. RATHER LIKE THE MARVELOUS GARDENS AROUND PALACES WHERE EVERY BLADE OF GRASS AND EVERY FLOWER IS CONTROLLED IN ITS GROWTH AND BLOOM, MADE TO PLEASE THE AESTHETIC SENSES; IN CONTRAST TO WILDERNESS PRESERVES WHERE NATURE EXULTS IN ITS OWN GROWTH. THE FOLK CRAFTSMANSHIP ALLOWS THE WOOD TO SPEAK, INDEED SING OUT, ITS OWN SHAPE AND TEXTURE AND FORM — ITS OWN DESIRE TO BE EXPRESSED.

IT IS APPROPRIATE TO MENTION HERE THE RUSSIAN SCULPTOR, SERGIE KONENKOV, WHOM FECHIN CONSIDERED THE GREATEST OF OUR TIME. KONENKOV WAS BORN (1874) IN A REMOTE BACK-

WOODS VILLAGE INTO A PEASANT FAMILY. HE GREW UP AMONG
TILLERS OF THE SOIL, LUMBERJACKS, CRAFTSMEN AND MASONS;
INWARDLY HE NEVER PARTED WITH THE PICK OR THE SHOVEL. HIS
PEASANT FAMILY RECOGNIZED THE BOY'S TALENTS AND DID ALL
THEY COULD TO GET HIM SOME EDUCATION. KONENKOV
AND FECHIN HAD DEEP FEELING FOR EACH OTHER AND FOR EACH
OTHER'S WORK. THEIR EMERGENCE AS GREAT ARTISTS STEMMED
FROM SIMILAR BACKGROUNDS. KONENKOV COULD TAKE MARBLE
OR WOOD AND MAKE IT SPEAK. HE PARTICULARLY LOVED TO USE
A TREE OR A ROOT AND HELP ITS OWN FANTASTIC "SOUL" TO
EMERGE. FECHIN WAS ALWAYS DEEPLY INFLUENCED BY KONENKOV
IN HIS WOOD WORK. THERE IS NO DOUBT THAT FECHIN WOULD
HAVE WANTED TO WELCOME KONENKOV INTO THE TAOS HOUSE
AND OFTEN THOUGHT OF HIM AS HE BUILT AND CARVED AND
COMMUNED WITH WOOD.

A FEW MORE FACTS SHOULD BE BROUGHT UP WHICH FIT INTO THE
HISTORICAL DEVELOPMENT OF ATTITUDES AND INFLUENCES WHICH
WERE PART OF FECHIN'S CHARACTER.

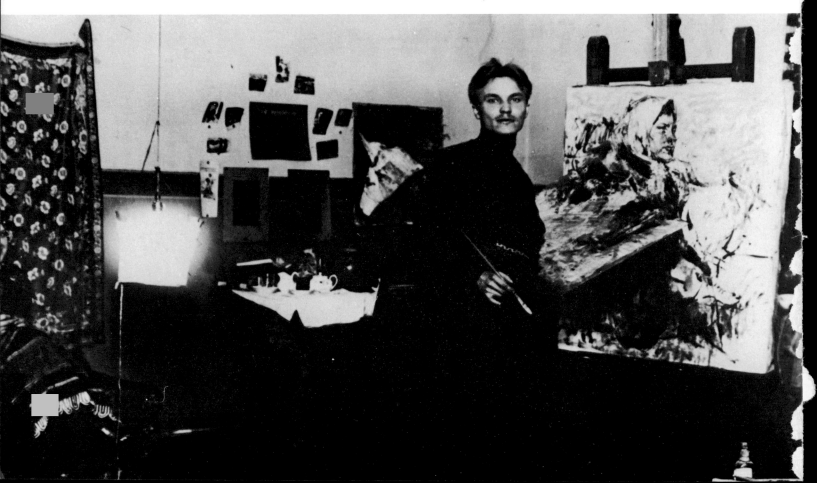

THERE WAS THE FOUNDING OF THE ART ACADEMY IN LENINGRAD IN 1757 WHICH WAS OF GREAT SIGNIFICANCE IN THE HISTORY OF RUSSIAN ARTS. IT RAPIDLY DEVELOPED INTO ONE OF THE LEADING ART SCHOOLS OF THE WORLD, ACHIEVING UNQUESTIONED AUTHORITY AND RECOGNITION. IT WAS THIS ACADEMY WHERE FECHIN FINISHED WITH THE TITLE OF "ARTIST."

THERE WERE NURTURING IDEAS AND INFLUENCES OF FAR-REACHING MINDS SUCH AS ALEXANDER SCRIABIN (1872-1915), THE FAMOUS COMPOSER, WHO ATTEMPTED TO TRANSFORM THE WORLD BY SYNTHESIZING THE ARTS, ACHIEVING A TOTAL EXPERIENCE. HOWEVER, IN HIS DAY THEATER DID NOT HAVE THE FREEDOM OF MECHANICAL AIDS (FOR SOUND, COLOR, ETC. EFFECTS) AND IT IS ONLY NOW THAT THERE ARE PERFORMANCES OF HIS WORK IN THE USSR CALLED "COSMO-MUSIC."

ANATOL LUNACHARSKY (1903), CRITIC, TRAVELER, FIRST COM-MISAR OF EDUCATION IN USSR SAID: "ART IS MAN'S EPIC SONG ABOUT HIMSELF AND HIS ENVIRONMENT. IT IS, ALL OF IT, ONE NEVER-ENDING LYRICAL AND FANTASTIC AUTOBIOGRAPHY OF THE HUMAN SPECIES."

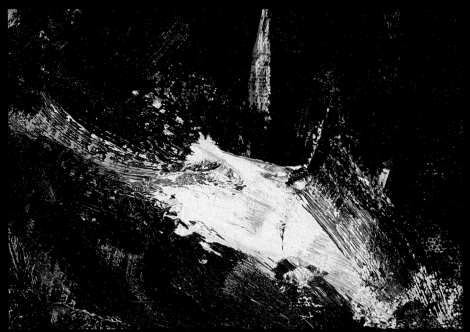

DETAIL FROM "RUSSIAN SINGER WITH FAN" — 48 x 33½, OIL ON CANVAS — NEW YORK, 1924-26.

THESE REPRODUCTIONS ARE A PART OF A FORTHCOMING BOOK FOCUSING ON FECHIN'S WORK WITH COLOR AND HIS UNUSUAL "SEING" ABILITY. DETAILS SIMILAR TO THE ONE ABOVE ARE SMALL SECTIONS (APPROXIMATELY 2½ X 3 INCHES) CAREFULLY SELECTED TO SHOW THE MANY BEAUTIFULLY BALANCED COMPOSITIONS WITHIN THE WHOLE OF A PAINTING. THE GOAL IS TO TRAVEL INTO THE PAINTINGS, TO EXPERIENCE THE VIBRANCY OF SINGING COLORS, TO LOVE EACH INCH OF CANVAS.

PHOTOGRAPHS BY GORDON ADAMS

MANICURE LADY — 28½ x 26½, OIL ON CANVAS — RUSSIA, 1917.

IN A DECREE OF 1918, LENIN DREW UP RULES FOR COLLECTING
AND PRESERVING HISTORIC MONUMENTS AND ARTS. TODAY SUCH
INSTITUTIONS AS THE TRETYAKOV GALLERY IN MOSCOW, THE
RUSSIAN MUSEUM IN LENINGRAD AND MANY PROVINCIAL
MUSEUMS HAVE EXTRAORDINARY COLLECTIONS OF OLD RUSSIAN
ART, WONDERFULLY RESTORED. THE RUBLEV MUSEUM OF
OLD RUSSIAN ART IN MOSCOW WAS OPENED ON THE 600TH
ANNIVERSARY OF ANDREY RUBLEV.

FECHIN PLAYING A ZITHER-LIKE
INSTRUMENT WHILE SINGING
WITH CLOSE FRIENDS IN RUSSIA.
OPPOSITE PAGE: CARVED HANGING
SIDEBOARD EXECUTED IN RUSSIA
SIMILAR TO ONE FECHIN CARVED
SO MANY YEARS LATER IN TAOS.

ENTIRE CITIES ARE NOW MADE INTO MUSEUMS. MONASTERY
COMPLEXES, SURROUNDED BY VILLAGES, ARE LIKE LIVING
MUSEUMS. ANCIENT BUILDINGS ARE BEING MOVED, WHOLE, TO
KIZHI ISLAND TO PRESERVE THEM IN ISOLATED SAFETY AWAY
FROM THE DESTRUCTIVENESS OF CITIES. ARTIST'S HOMES AND
STUDIOS ARE BECOMING MUSEUMS — NOT MERELY HISTORICAL
SITES OF POLITICAL MOMENTS. KONENKOV'S STUDIO AND HOME
IN MOSCOW IS ONE SUCH EXAMPLE, FULL OF HIS WORK — FROM
FURNITURE TO HIS LAST UNFINISHED PIECES OF MAGNIFICENT
SCULPTURES.

FECHIN WAS BORN IN 1881 INTO A SIMPLE FAMILY OF CRAFTSMEN
LIVING IN KAZAN ON THE SHORES OF THE VOLGA RIVER, THE
FOREST HEARTLAND. ALONG THE RIVER WHERE THE SHIPS AND

BOATS DOCK, THE IMPRESSION IS OF A SEAPORT, THE RIVER BEING INCREDIBLY BROAD, DEEP, AND ABUNDANT WITH FISH. KAZAN WAS ONE OF THE LAST OF THE TARTAR KHANATES (REMNANTS OF THE CONQUERING GOLDEN HORDE) AND WAS LIBERATED IN 1552 BY IVAN III. KAZAN WAS ALWAYS ONE OF THE IMPORTANT CITIES ON THE VOLGA FOR RIVER TRADE AND HAS ONE OF THE OLDEST UNIVERSITIES.

HIS FATHER CAME FROM ARZAMAS, WHICH WAS A VERY WEALTHY TRADING CENTER WHERE PEOPLE BUILT MANY FINE CHURCHES AND OTHER DWELLINGS. THE TOWN ABOUNDED WITH FINE CRAFTSMEN TO GILD AND CARVE THE ICONOSTASIS, PAINT ICONS AND DO CONSTRUCTION WORK OF ALL KINDS AS THE TOWN GREW. IVAN FECHIN LEARNED MANY OF THESE CRAFTS AS A BOY. UPON GROWING UP HE MOVED TO THE CITY OF KAZAN AND MARRIED THE DAUGHTER OF A LOCAL BUILDING CONTRACTOR. HIS BRIDE CAME FROM THE CITY OF KOSTROMA — ANOTHER PLACE FULL OF FINE BUILDINGS AND BUSY TRADE. HE OPENED A SHOP OF HIS OWN AND AT FIRST, HAD A GREAT DEAL OF WORK. SO THE EARLY YEARS OF LIFE WERE VERY COMFORTABLE FOR SMALL NICOLAI AND HE SPENT MUCH TIME IN THE ACTIVE CRAFTSHOP LEARNING ALL ABOUT CONSTRUCTION, CARPENTRY, CARVING, AND GILDING.

NICOLAI'S EARLIEST CHILDHOOD MEMORY WAS THE STORY HIS MOTHER OFTEN REMINISCED ABOUT, WHICH FITS INTO HIS PATTERN OF DEVELOPMENT LIKE A PIECE OF THE ICONOSTASIS. WHEN HE WAS ABOUT FOUR YEARS OLD HE WAS VERY ILL, PROBABLY OF MENINGITIS (A FATAL SICKNESS IN THOSE DAYS). THE MOTHER WEPT OVER THE CHILD AND FOR WEEKS HE HARDLY SHOWED ANY SIGNS OF LIFE.

THE BEST DOCTORS AVAILABLE GAVE UP, CLAIMING THAT EVEN IF HE SURVIVED HE WOULD BE INCAPACITATED. THE PARENTS WOULD

NOT GIVE UP. THERE WAS IN KAZAN A FAMOUS AND POPULAR ICON CALLED THE ICON OF TICHINSKOYA, MOTHER OF GOD, AND IT WAS CONSIDERED TO BE MIRACULOUS. THERE WERE MANY LEGENDS OF CURES ATTRIBUTED TO IT. IT WAS A LARGE ICON AND TOOK TWO MEN TO CARRY IT.

AS WAS THE CUSTOM, THERE WAS A CEREMONY OF BRINGING IT TO THE HOUSE, WITH MANY PRAYERS, INCENSE, POMP. IT HAD TO BE PASSED OVER THE BODY OF THE AILING ONE, THREE TIMES. SURPRISINGLY, AT THE FIRST "TOUCH" OF THE ICON, THE BOY SHOWED THE FIRST SIGNS OF LIFE AFTER TWO WEEKS OF COMA AND SOON RECOVERED ENTIRELY. UNDOUBTEDLY, WE WOULD SAY NOW THAT THE ILLNESS HAD RUN ITS COURSE AND THE CRISIS OF RECOVERY COINCIDED WITH THE ICON'S VISIT. FECHIN WAS A SKEPTIC IN SUCH MATTERS, BUT LATER IN LIFE HE WOULD REMEMBER THE OCCURRENCE, LAUGH AND SAY HE HAD TO BE HEALED IN ORDER TO FULFILL HIS DESTINY AS AN ARTIST!

NICOLAI'S FATHER GAVE HIM MUCH ATTENTION AND DREAMED HE WOULD BECOME HIS ASSISTANT. THE WORK REQUIRED A VERY SKILLED DRAUGHTSMAN FOR THE WHOLE STRUCTURE OF A NEW CHURCH WAS BASED ON THESE DETAILED DRAWINGS. IVAN HIMSELF COULD NOT DRAW AND THEREFORE WAS GREATLY IMPRESSED WHEN THE SMALL BOY SHOWED HIS ABILITY TO DRAW BY THE TIME HE WAS ABOUT SIX YEARS OLD. IVAN WAS A HUMBLE MAN, LOVED HIS WORK PASSIONATELY AND WAS KIND TO A FAULT. HE NEVER CALCULATED THE COSTS OF HIS WORKS PROPERLY, SUFFERED LOSSES, AND GOT INTO DEBT. SO STARTED A TIME OF NEED FOR THE FAMILY. IVAN TRIED TO FIND WORK IN VARIOUS VILLAGES AND WAS TOO OFTEN AWAY FROM HOME. DURING SUMMERS HE WOULD TAKE NICOLAI WITH HIM AND THE CHILD LOVED THESE TRIPS INTO THE COUNTRY, INTO THE DEPTHS OF THE FOREST LAND.

WHEN THIRTEEN YEARS OLD, NICOLAI EARNED HIS FIRST MONEY FOR HIS OWN WORK. HE MADE A DRAWING FOR THE BUILDING OF A NEW SHRINE AND RECEIVED TEN RUBLES FOR THIS COMMISSION. THUS FECHIN BEGAN AS A "BUILDER."

THE SAME YEAR A NEW ART SCHOOL OPENED IN KAZAN, A SCHOOL OF PAINTING, ARCHITECTURE AND SCULPTURE. IT WAS A BRANCH OF THE ART ACADEMY IN LENINGRAD AND OFFERED A SIX-YEAR COURSE IN ART, INCLUDING A REGULAR HIGH SCHOOL CURRICULUM OF EDUCATION. A VERY DEMOCRATIC SCHOOL, IT WAS ORGANIZED FOR THE POOR, NOT THE RICH. IVAN, STILL DREAMING THAT NICOLAI WOULD BECOME AN ARTIST, ENROLLED HIM IN THE SCHOOL.

NOW NICOLAI BEGAN HIS LIFE AWAY FROM HIS PARENTS. HIS FATHER LEFT KAZAN LOOKING FOR WORK; HIS MOTHER WENT BACK TO HER PARENTS IN KOSTRAMA. YEARS LATER, WHEN NICOLAI WAS ALREADY AN ARTIST, HE WAS ABLE TO GET HIS PARENTS TOGETHER AGAIN. THE YEARS IN THE KAZAN SCHOOL WERE PRODUCTIVE; LIFE OF A STUDENT WAS POOR AND FULL OF STRUGGLES, BUT THE EXCITEMENT OF ART AND STUDY LEFT NO TIME FOR ANYTHING ELSE. SUMMERS WERE SPENT IN THE COUNTRY. AN UNCLE HAD A SMALL TURPENTINE FACTORY IN A LITTLE VILLAGE (KUSHNIYA) SOME HUNDRED MILES FROM KAZAN. IT WAS A VERY WILD SECTION, SPARSELY SETTLED PRIMARILY BY CHEREMISS TRIBES, UNTOUCHED BY CIVILIZATION. THE LIFE OF THE NATIVES WITH THEIR MYSTERIOUS PAGAN RITES IN THE DEPTHS OF THE FOREST WHICH NICOLAI OBSERVED, DEVELOPED IN HIM A LOVE FOR EVERYTHING THAT PERTAINED TO NATURE.

WHEN 19 YEARS OLD, UPON GRADUATION FROM THE KAZAN ART SCHOOL, NICOLAI WAS ACCEPTED INTO THE ACADEMY OF ART IN LENINGRAD. SUMMERS WERE STILL SPENT IN THE COUNTRY — WITH HIS UNCLE IN KUSHNIYA, WITH ANOTHER RELATIVE WHO LIVED ON THE BANKS OF THE VOLGA RIVER OR, TWICE, WITH AN ENGINEER-GEOLOGIST FRIEND GOING INTO SIBERIA. THE LATTER LONG TRIPS WERE A WONDROUS ADVENTURE FOR NICOLAI AND HE WAS ENCHANTED WITH THE WILDERNESS OF SIBERIA. AFTER HIS GRADUATION FROM THE ACADEMY AND A TRIP TO EUROPE, NICOLAI SETTLED IN KAZAN, TEACHING IN THE ART SCHOOL AND LIVING IN A WONDERFUL STUDIO AT THE SCHOOL.

THIS STUDIO BECAME A FOCAL POINT FOR STUDENTS AND COLLEAGUES ALIKE. AS ONE STUDENT (POPOVA) WROTE: "... THE WHOLE STUDIO WAS LIKE A RARE MUSEUM ... THE ROOM HUNG WITH RUGS, COLORFUL FABRICS AND FILLED WITH FURNITURE THAT FECHIN HAD, HIMSELF, BUILT AND CARVED ... WHIMSICAL CARVING WITH WHICH THE SIDEBOARD WAS DECORATED, A CHAIR, A MIRROR FRAME AND A WARDROBE WITH INLAID WORK OF COPPER AND SEMI-PRECIOUS STONES ... EVERYTHING AS IF IN A BEAUTIFUL FAIRY TALE." HERE GATHERED MUSICIANS, POETS, ARTISTS, STUDENTS — OTHER CREATIVE PEOPLE OF DIVERSE PROFESSIONS — WITH A DEEP FEELING OF CAMARADERIE.

THE REVOLUTION DISRUPTED THE RHYTHM OF LIFE; FAMINE AND SICKNESS SWEPT THROUGH THE CITIES. ARTISTS WERE TREATED AS WELL AS WAS POSSIBLE, BUT THE HARDSHIPS WERE STRENUOUS FOR EVERYBODY. DUE TO FECHIN'S POSITION AS A TEACHER-ARTIST, THERE WAS AN ORDER OUT TO PROTECT HIM. NICOLAI WAS MARRIED BY THEN AND HIS HOME WAS OUT IN THE COUNTRY, IN A FOREST AREA NEAR THE VOLGA SOME THIRTY MILES OR MORE BY TRAIN FROM KAZAN. THIS BECAME A REFUGE, WITH FISH FROM THE RIVER, CHICKENS, A VEGETABLE GARDEN AND EVENTUALLY A COW. PROBLEMS AND WORRIES WERE MANY, BUT THE COUNTRY LIFE WASN'T BAD AND CERTAINLY FAR HEALTHIER THAN ANY CITY.

THE DECISION TO LEAVE THE MOTHERLAND WAS VERY DIFFICULT FOR NICOLAI. ILL HEALTH, THE DEATH (FROM CHOLERA) OF HIS PARENTS, THE INVITATION FROM THE UNITED STATES TO COME FOR EXHIBITIONS IN AMERICA, THE INSISTANCE FROM HIS WIFE TO GO — FINALLY PERSUADED HIM TO MAKE THE MOVE. SOME OF FECHIN'S STUDENTS WERE IN GOOD POSITIONS IN THE NEW GOVERNMENT AND PAPERS WERE OBTAINED FOR THE BIG LEAP INTO THE UNKNOWN. DURING THE HOT SUMMER OF 1923 FECHIN WENT ON HIS BIGGEST ADVENTURE. . .

LIFE IN THE BIGGEST CITY, NEW YORK, WAS SUCCESSFUL IN TERMS OF WORK, BUT THE LONGING FOR THE WILDERNESS AND COUNTRY LIFE GREW INCESSANTLY. AFTER FOUR YEARS, THE MOVE WAS MADE TO TAOS, NEW MEXICO. A PLACE WAS BOUGHT AND TOTALLY REBUILT BETWEEN 1927-33 — THE AMERICAN HOME. THE AMOUNT OF WORK THAT WENT INTO THE PLACE WAS AWESOME. FECHIN WAS ENCHANTED BY THE INDIAN LAND, THE DIFFERENT CULTURES, THE MOUNTAINS, THE BRILLIANT LIGHT OF THE HIGH PLATEAU. THE DIVERSITY OF PEOPLE (INDIAN, SPANISH, A VARIETY OF ANGLOS) REMINDED HIM OF KAZAN WITH ITS MANY TRIBES AND CULTURES. THE MOUNTAINS REMINDED HIM OF THE CAUCASUS (THE SOVIET REPUBLIC OF GEORGIA).

HE FIRST REBUILT A SMALL SEPARATE BUILDING INTO A SPACIOUS STUDIO WITH A LARGE NORTH WINDOW — AND AS LONG AS THE LIGHT WAS GOOD, HE PAINTED. WHEN THE LIGHT FAILED HE BECAME A BUILDER, CARPENTER, CARVER, SCULPTOR. HE JOYED IN HIS WORK, THE LABOR WAS STIMULATING. THERE WAS A DEEP SATISFACTION IN BRINGING THIS MUCH OF HIS MOTHERLAND TO A FOREIGN BUT SEEMINGLY FAMILIAR CORNER OF THE WORLD. INDEED, HE WAS COMPELLED, DRIVEN, TO REPRODUCE SUCH AN ENVIRONMENT WITHIN WHICH HIS SOUL FELT AT HOME AND HIS PAINTING FLOURISHED.

HE BROUGHT DOWN SMALL ASPENS AND SPRUCE FROM THE
MOUNTAINS AND PLANTED THEM AROUND THE BUILDINGS. AFTER
HE LEFT TAOS, THE ASPENS DIED FROM LACK OF CARE, BUT
THE SPRUCE TREES REMAIN TOWERING IN HIS MEMORY. INSIDE
THE HOUSE THERE ARE THE REMINDERS OF HIS KAZAN STUDIO...
THE FINE PRAYER RUG FROM THE NEAR EAST, THE HUGE PAISLEY
SHAWL, A COUPLE OF LITTLE BOXES WITH METAL WORK
AND STONES, THE EMBROIDERED RUSSIAN TOWELS, A FEW
FAVORITE WOVEN DRAPES. THERE IS THE HANGING SHELF SO
SIMILAR TO THE ONE WHICH WAS IN KAZAN. IT IS ALL THERE —
EXPANDED, DEVELOPED, ADAPTED TO THE ADOBE BUILDING,
THE MUD WHICH WAS SO RESPONSIVE TO THE HAND AND WHICH
DELIGHTED THE IMAGINATION OF THE BUILDER. HE WAS
ENCHANTED WITH ADOBE, THE HOUSES THAT GREW OUT OF THE
GROUND AND CHANGED COLOR AS THE SUN MOVED.

PART OF THE JOY OF WORKING WAS SCULPTING IN WOOD AND IN CLAY. RUSSIAN SCULPTURE HAS A VERY LONG HISTORY, THE ORIGINS LOST IN THE MISTS OF TIME. IT WAS INTIMATELY CONNECTED WITH "FOLK ART," FULL OF EXHUBERANT IMAGINATION AND THE MATERIAL USED WAS USUALLY WOOD. FECHIN THOUGHT OF HIS FRIEND, KONENKOV, AND JOINED HIM IN THE ADVENTURE OF SCULPTING. HE USED LOCAL FIREWOOD, SELECTING PIECES OF PINON AND COTTONWOOD FOR THEIR INTRIGUING CHARACTERISTICS, THE WOOD CALLING OUT ITS DESIRE TO EXPRESS ITSELF. FECHIN DID THIS WORK ONLY FOR HIS OWN PLEASURE, WITH NO INTENTION OF SELLING ANY. THE PIECES WERE MOSTLY HIS CHILDREN OF FANTASY — ONLY A FEW WERE PORTRAIT STYLE. LATER, IN CALIFORNIA, HE ALSO ENJOYED CERAMICS, MAKING WONDERFUL PIECES FOR HIS OWN PLEASURE.

FECHIN MADE SMALL, QUICK PENCIL SKETCHES OF ARCHITECTURAL DESIGN, INDIVIDUAL FORMS, IDEAS FOR WINDOWS, DOORS, FURNITURE. A ROUGH CARDBOARD MODEL OF THE HOUSE WAS MADE, BUT NO SCALE DRAWINGS OR COMPLETED DESIGNS TO BE COPIED IN ACTUAL CONSTRUCTION. AS THE BUILDING PROGRESSED THE IDEAS CHANGED, GREW AND DEVELOPED SPONTANEOUSLY. EVERY DOORWAY, OPENING AND WINDOW GIVES THE VIEWER A BALANCED COMPOSITION. IT IS THE SAME DEEP SENSE OF HARMONY AND COMPOSITION ONE SEES IN HIS PAINTINGS.

IT SHOULD BE MENTIONED HERE, THAT IN ORDER TO FINISH THE ART ACADEMY IN LENINGRAD, ALL STUDENTS HAD TO LEARN AS MUCH ABOUT ARCHITECTURE AS AN ARCHITECT, AND AS MUCH ABOUT ANATOMY AS THOUGH THEY WERE IN MEDICAL SCHOOL. THE SAME THOROUGHNESS APPLIED TO THE STUDY OF THEATER DESIGN AND CHEMISTRY. THUS, IT BECOMES EASIER TO COMPREHEND HOW FECHIN COULD VISUALIZE THESE MYRIAD SHAPES AND SPACES AND ANTICIPATE THEIR IMPACT FROM ALL POSSIBLE VANTAGE POINTS.

STEPPING INTO THE FECHIN HOUSE IS AN EXTRAORDINARY EXPERIENCE. EVERYWHERE ONE LOOKS, CARVED UNDULATING FORMS ALMOST CRY OUT TO BE TOUCHED TO FULLY KNOW THEIR BEING. THE BALANCE AND HARMONY ARE FELT AS WELL AS SEEN — THE HOUSE "SINGS" FOR YOU. A RUSSIAN HOUSE EVOLVED OUT OF NEW MEXICO MUD. A BLACKSMITH, A CARPENTER... INDIANS, SPANISH, AND ANGLOS, WORKED HARD AND HAPPILY ALONGSIDE THE MASTER ARTIST.

PREDOMINANTLY WHAT ONE FEELS ON ENTERING THE HOUSE IS THE ALL-PERVADING SENSE OF LOVE AND JOY IN THE PROCESS OF CREATING IT. THE LABOR IS NOT PONDEROUS, BUT FULL OF ZEST AND WHIMSY. ONE IS FILLED WITH ADVENTURE, SUSPENSE — THERE IS ALWAYS MORE FOR THE EYE TO SEE, FOR THE MIND TO GRASP, FOR THE HEART TO ABSORB. THIS WAS THE ENVIRONMENT IN WHICH FECHIN WISHED HIS PAINTINGS TO BE SEEN. PERHAPS THE HOUSE IN TAOS WAS RATHER LIKE AN ICONOSTASIS AND THE PAINTINGS HIS "ICONS"!

AT THE AGE OF SEVENTY, FECHIN LAMENTED HOW "I AM NOT ABLE TO WORK ALMOST TWENTY-FOUR HOURS A DAY AS I ONCE COULD." HE ALSO SAID, "AN ARTIST SHOULD WORK EVERY DAY WITH EVERYTHING THAT IS AT HAND...IT IS NECESSARY TO EXERCISE THE HAND AND THE EYE THE SAME WAY IT IS NECESSARY FOR A MUSICIAN TO EXERCISE EVERY DAY HIS HEARING AND HIS HANDS." FECHIN LIVED FOR ART.

WITHOUT IT HE COULD NOT IMAGINE LIFE — FOR HIM THE GOAL OF LIFE WAS CREATIVE WORK. HE WOULD SAY, WHILE TEACHING IN KAZAN, "ART DEMANDS THE WHOLE PERSON AND FOR THE WHOLE OF LIFE. DON'T THINK THAT YOU ARE ALREADY ARTISTS IF YOU ARE STANDING ONLY ON ONE LITTLE STEP...THE STRIVING MUST BE HIGH, TO HEAVEN ITSELF." BUT HE ALSO SAID, MUCH LATER IN CALIFORNIA, "TAKE CARE TO KEEP YOUR MIND OPEN TO ALL THAT IS WONDROUS. TO LOVE ART IS NECESSARY, BUT TO BECOME ITS SLAVE IS BAD, SINCE YOU LOSE YOUR JUDGEMENT. ...ART ENCLOSED IN ITSELF DIES..."

FECHIN LOVED FINE HAND TOOLS AND
HAD AN EXTENSIVE COLLECTION OF
ENGLISH AND GERMAN CARVING CHISELS,
WOOD AND LEATHER MALLETS OF DIF-
FERENT SIZES, MANY SHARPENING STONES,
A HAND GRINDING WHEEL, AXES, THE
LARGE ADZE, HAND DRILLS, AND SAWS. HE
USED A SMALL ANVIL FOR METAL WORK
(HE MADE ALL THE HARDWARE, LANTERNS,
LIGHT FIXTURES TOGETHER WITH MR.
HINDE, A TAOS BLACKSMITH). THE ROOM
NEXT TO THE STUDIO BECAME A VERY
COMPLETE CARPENTRY AND CARVING SHOP.
HE KEPT ALL HIS TOOLS (AND PAINT
BRUSHES) IN PERFECT SHAPE AND HIS STUDIO AND SHOP WERE
ALWAYS IN AN ORDERLY, READY-TO-WORK CONDITION. ONLY
CHISELS WERE USED IN HIS WOODCARVING — CHIPCARVING
TECHNIQUES AND KNIVES WERE NOT EMPLOYED. ALL SANDING
WORK WAS DONE BY HAND — THERE WERE NO ELECTRIC
MACHINES. HE ONCE RENTED AN ELECTRIC LATHE, MADE SOME
SPINDLES ON IT AND SOON RETURNED IT — DISLIKING THE NOISE
AND LOSS OF CONTACT WITH THE WOOD.

FECHIN NEVER PAINTED BY ARTIFICIAL LIGHT. HE NEEDED GOOD
NORTH LIGHT AND WORKED FROM EARLY MORNING UNTIL THE
LIGHT BEGAN FAILING IN THE AFTERNOON. THIS GAVE HIM THE
LATE AFTERNOON AND EVENING HOURS FOR SCULPTING, CARVING,
BUILDING, GARDENING. THUS, NATURALLY, DURING THE WINTERS
HE SPENT MORE TIME IN CARVING AND BUILDING FURNITURE.

HE MADE SEVERAL PORTRAITS IN CLAY WHICH HE HIMSELF CAST IN
PLASTER. THESE HE INTENDED TO MAKE INTO BRONZES, BUT
THERE WAS NO FOUNDRY NEARER THAN NEW YORK AT THE TIME,
SO HE SET THEM ASIDE. THE BRONZES WERE MADE AFTER HIS
DEATH. IN CALIFORNIA HE EXPERIMENTED WITH MORTICIAN'S
WAX AND MADE SEVERAL SMALL FIGURES WHICH WERE ALSO CAST
IN BRONZE MUCH LATER. BUT, ABOVE ALL, HE LOVED SCULPTING
IN WOOD, SELECTING INTERESTING PIECES FROM THE PILE OF
FIREWOOD IN THE YARD WHICH WAS BURNED IN STOVES FOR
HEATING THE HOUSE...PINON, COTTONWOOD, PINE. THE WOOD
HEADS AND FIGURES WERE MOSTLY IMAGINARY, NO MODELS WERE
USED, THE WOOD ITSELF INDICATED WHAT THE SUBJECT WOULD
BE. HE WOULD ADD TOUCHES OF COLOR WITH TEMPERA, BUT
WOULD NOT PUT ANY OTHER FINISH ON THE PIECES EXCEPT HAND
RUBBING. AT TIMES HE USED A TORCH TO ACCENT HAIR OR FACE
OR BRING OUT THE GRAIN IN THE WOOD. (ONE WONDERFUL
EXAMPLE IS THE NEGRO BOY'S HEAD IN THE STARK MUSEUM IN
ORANGE, TEXAS). THE OUTLINE OF THE FACE OR FIGURE WAS
FIRST LIGHTLY DRAWN ON THE WOOD AND THE CARVING BEGUN.

FOR FURNITURE MAKING AND FOR THE INTERIOR OF THE HOUSE, THE RANDALL LUMBER MILL IN TAOS SUPPLIED HIM WITH BOARDS, BEAMS AND WHATEVER HE DESIRED. IF THE LUMBER WAS NOT AT HAND, QUANTITIES WERE ORDERED FOR HIM. THE WOOD USED WAS MOSTLY FINISHED, CLEAR, WHITE PINE — BEAUTIFUL THICK BOARDS DIFFICULT TO FIND TODAY. LATER HE BEGAN TO USE FINE, CLEAR POPLAR BOARDS, FINDING THIS A HARDER WOOD, EASIER FOR MORE DELICATE CARVING DETAIL.

ALL BOARDS AND BEAMS WERE FIRST FINISHED WITH AN ADZE. FECHIN LIKED THE TEXTURE AND FINISH THUS OBTAINED. HE BECAME INCREDIBLY ADEPT WITH THE ADZE, GETTING A BROAD, EVEN STROKE THAT STILL DELIGHTS WOOD-WORKERS. THE BOARDS WERE CUT TO FIT THE FORMS OF THE FURNITURE (DOORS, WINDOWS, ETC.) AND DESIGNS DRAWN ON THE SEPARATE PIECES. THE CARVING WAS DONE AND THEN THOROUGHLY SANDED BY HAND USING VARIOUS WEIGHTS OF SANDPAPER TO GET A FINE, SOFT FINISH. FECHIN LIKED THINGS TO BE TOUCHABLE, SOFT-EDGED. HE OFTEN USED A SMALL GASOLINE TORCH TO DARKEN AREAS AND ACHIEVE A LEATHER-LIKE TONE AND QUALITY. THE TORCH WAS MOVED CONSTANTLY LIKE A BRUSH, AVOIDING SPOTTING OR CHARRING. THE BOARDS WERE LIGHTLY STAINED FOR UNIFORMITY OF TONE — THE STAIN BEING HIGHLY DILUTED WITH TURPENTINE, WIPED ON, NOT PAINTED ON, THE NATURAL WOOD ALWAYS SHOWING THROUGH. ON SOME MORE DEEPLY CUT DESIGNS, ASHES WERE SPRINKLED ON THROUGH A FINE SIEVE AND THEN BRUSHED OFF, LEAVING ASH IN CREVICES FOR ACCENT. THIS WAS NOT AN ATTEMPT TO "ANTIQUE," BUT MERELY TO ACHIEVE A TEXTURE AND TONE HE DESIRED AND UNIFY THE INDIVIDUAL PIECES INTO A HARMONIOUS WHOLE.

THE LAST JOB WAS TO RUB ON HARD FLOOR WAX, LET IT SIT A FEW HOURS AND POLISH LIGHTLY WITH A FLANNEL OR WOOL CLOTH. THIS SIMPLE FINISH PROVED ITS WORTH MORE THAN FIFTY YEARS LATER, WHEN, AFTER ALL THOSE YEARS OF NEGLECT AND DUST, THE WOODWORK NEEDED ONLY ANOTHER APPLICATION OF WAX AND A LITTLE BUFFING TO MAKE THE WOOD SING OUT IN ITS ORIGINAL BEAUTY.

FECHIN CARVING TAMARA — THIS
PIECE OF WOOD SCULPTURE RELATES
TO THE WORK OF THE RUSSIAN
ARTIST M.I. VRUBEL (1865-1905).
FECHIN WAS AFFECTED VERY MUCH
BY THIS MAN'S WORK — EVEN USING
VRUBEL'S PAINTING "TAMARA" (1890)
AS THE MODEL FOR THIS UNFINISHED
PIECE. HIS COUNTRYMAN'S WORK
LEFT AN INDELIBLE IMPRINT ON HIS
IMAGINATION.

DRIFTWOOD ROOT

ACCENTUATED BY CARVING AND USED AS A MODEL FOR TWO DRAWINGS AND THE OIL PAINTING "DRIFTWOOD MONSTER"

Tamara

NICOLAI'S FATHER

Two Pilgrims — These two figures are a tribute to the work of Sergei Konenkov (1874-1971) whom Fechin considered to be the greatest sculptor of his time.

HEAD OF MONGOLIAN GIRL   PAN (IN THE STYLE OF VRUBEL)

Nude

MONGOLIAN BOY

SANDRA

EYA